Nice Guys

and

Players

Becoming the Man Women Want

Nice Guys and Players

Becoming the Man Women Want

Rom Wills

E.R.L. Publishing

Nice Guys and Players
Becoming the Man Women Want

Copyright © 2000
By
Rom Wills

Cover Design by Rom Wills
Cover Photo by Ronald Beverly

Printed in the United States of America
Fourth Printing

E.R.L. Publishing
P.O. Box 4071
Arlington, VA 22204
erlpublishing@aol.com

Library of Congress Control Number 00-092579

ISBN 0-9655682-3-7

Acknowledgements

I extend my sincerest gratitude to the following:

The Creator through whom all blessings flow.

My soulmate Althea for her love and support.

My family members who have always believed in me, especially my grandmother who has been a rock in my life; my mother for unconditionally believing in me; and my sister for sharing her cookies.

My friends for their support. It's too many to name everybody but you all know who you are.

Yao Nyamekye Morris for his invaluable insights into the spiritual nature of intimate relationships.

All the men and women who have shared their relationship experiences with me. All of your insights made this book possible.

To Althea

Table of Contents

Introduction

Larry and Christa have dated for three months. Larry is nice and respectful to Christa. He helps her grocery shop and makes sure her car is always clean and filled with gas. He takes her to the restaurant of her choice. Larry calls when he says he will. He never gets mad if Christa says she's going to hang out with the girls. Larry even gives her spending money. Larry has a good job, clean apartment in a good neighborhood, and a dependable car. He dresses cleanly and appropriately despite being somewhat pudgy. He volunteers to mentor young fatherless boys and is viewed as a role model by many people. Christa's parents think Larry would make a great son-in-law. What's missing from Larry and Christa's relationship is they have yet to be intimate. Christa told Larry she wanted to wait until they were married before having sex. Larry, although turned on by Christa, understands and doesn't pressure her. After one date, Larry kisses Christa and goes home thinking he has found a great woman. He dreams about the day they will be married. He fantasizes about how he will one day make love to her slowly and romantically.

Once Larry is gone, Christa pages Patrick. Patrick answers the page. Then Christa invites him to come over to her apartment despite the fact it's after midnight. When Patrick arrives he is wearing an oversized shirt, baggy jeans, and boots. He looks like a model right out of a hip-hop magazine. Christa has on a red teddy. As soon as Patrick gets in the door he starts taking off his clothes. Christa gets hot over the sight of Patrick's hardbody. Patrick wastes no time in having sex with Christa. He takes off her teddy and starts having sex with her right on the couch. The sex is hot and intense. Christa feels like she is in heaven. After the sex Patrick gets up, puts on his clothes and leaves. No foreplay, no afterplay, barely a kiss. Christa doesn't mind because she always screams out in orgasm with Patrick.

Scenarios like the one I just described happen everyday. Most men are either like Larry who is nice and kind to women or like Patrick who uses women for sex. Most men are either nice guys or players. Nice guys are largely ignored by women and when they do manage to get into a relationship, in many cases their time and generosity are taken advantage of. Players, on the other hand, get plenty of attention from women. Players can act anyway they please and get away with it because the majority of women want them. Both the nice guy and the player face significant problems when trying to find the right woman.

The problems nice guys have are obvious. Women simply don't see them. A woman will walk into a room with 90 nice guys and 10 players and only notice the players. Nice guys wonder why they don't get more attention. They read the books and articles about how women want sensitive men just like them. They hear women complain about how they have been mistreated by players and yet these women constantly go after players. After a while, many good men begin to withdraw from the dating scene. They become alone and bitter. Some even become players and treat women poorly.

The problems players face are not as obvious. After all, they get plenty of women. Many players have women approach them on the street. Women buy them clothes, loan them their cars, and let them live rent-free in their apartments. If women are not doing this then they are rushing over to be with the player whenever he wants them. The player seems like he has control. To a nice guy this must seem like paradise. This is not the case.

Players are human. No matter how many women

a player is able to get there's always one woman who'll reject him. She's the woman the player will fall in love with. No matter what he does she will not seriously consider him as a mate. Another scenario is when a woman is using the player for sex. Using the above example, Christa has no intentions of being serious with Patrick. She wants to marry Larry and maybe keep Patrick on the side. The problem is that Patrick is starting to feel something for Christa but she sees him as a sex partner and not a viable candidate for a long-term relationship. Patrick feels used and wonders why Christa doesn't appreciate him for anything other than sex.

Someone reading this may consider Christa to be mean, deceitful, and manipulative. She is in a way. Let's, however, break this down. Christa has one man to take care of her emotional needs: Larry. Larry is steady, dependable, and would make a good husband. Larry, however, doesn't turn on Christa physically. Patrick takes care of Christa's physical needs but is not dependable and is emotionally distant. The ideal man for Christa would be dependable like Larry and physically appealing like Patrick. Someone reading this may think this is a fantasy but it is not.

Women, and men as well, must be satisfied mentally as well as physically. This is especially true for women. This affects how a woman chooses a man and the nature of that relationship. Typically a man will only partly satisfy a woman because of these two needs. To fully satisfy a woman a man has to have both the characteristics of a nice guy and of a player. A man must become balanced between the two.

This book discusses steps to be taken by nice guys to become more physically appealing and steps to be taken by the player to become more emotionally appealing. This book will further discuss steps to be taken even after balance has been achieved.

People may wonder why I'm writing this book. The reason is simple. Male/female relationships are in a crisis state. Men and women are at war with each other. There are many casualties in this war. Many people have had their heads messed up. There have even been deaths. The main casualties are the children. While mommy and daddy are playing games the children are being neglected and hurt. The abuse of many children has its roots in this conflict. I couldn't sit by and do nothing.

I address this book to men. Not to say that women cannot read and learn from what's in this book. I address this book to men because many of the books on male/female relationships are addressed to ladies. The ladies are eating up these books and becoming empowered. They are doing so much to try and improve the state of relationships. I applaud their efforts. The problem is only one side of the issue is being addressed. So what if the ladies make themselves more appealing to men. So what if they work on bad attitudes and poor appearances. So what if they adjust their standards from wanting a high powered attorney to wanting a hardworking construction worker. For relationships to improve both men and women must get their acts together.

This book is for the men who do all those nice things for women only to watch them fall for the player. It is for the man who can get all the women except for the one he actually wants. I understand both these positions. In my life I have been both nice guy and player.

I don't have a Ph.D. I'm a man who has seen a lot in life. My greatest qualification to write about relationships is my experience. I have dated women from all over the world. Women old and young have confided in me. As they shared their experiences I have learned a lot and feel compelled to share what I have learned. It is my sincere desire that my perspective will help many good, hardworking men find the happiness they deserve.

The Choice

Most men think women are not interested in them. A man remembers all the times he's been rejected and ignored by women. Some men have done everything to attract women, but have failed miserably. In reality, most men, nice or otherwise, fail to attract women. Other men succeed most of the time. What makes some succeed while others fail? The ones who succeed, consciously or subconsciously, realize the secret to attracting women. I will now share that secret with you. Please read, reread, underline, highlight, and study what is about to follow.

The Secret

One day, a friend of mine I'll call Jim decided to tell me the secret of his success with women. Jim

17

attracted women like manure attracts flies. Women would quite literally camp out on his front lawn to see him and it wasn't even his house. He lived with his mother until he got married. Jim wasn't rich. He didn't have his own car. Jim would have women chase after him. The irony was you could never call him a player. I have known him since we were ten and I have never heard him use a pickup line with a woman. Not once. My success with women when I was young was never anywhere near his. So one day, after I got him sufficiently drunk, Jim decided to tell me the secret of his success with women. After he told me I asked, "That's it?" Jim replied, "Yeah, that's it. Gimme another beer." Just like that I knew the answer. Of course it took me a couple of years to master the concept, but hopefully it will take you a couple of weeks.

What's the secret? The secret is simple. **Women choose the men.** Sounds simple doesn't it? Well it is simple. Remembering those four words will get you more dating choices than you can handle. Mastering the concept behind those words will save you time, money, and heartbreak. The only time you will be without companionship is when you don't feel like being bothered. Women, in most cases, know exactly what they want in a man. They don't always end up with the men they want, but they still know. Women know who can turn them on and who cannot.

The Choice

Many women have told me they can take one look at a man and know whether or not they will date him. If a woman doesn't **choose** a man there is nothing he can do to win her heart. All the money, looks, prestige, charm, or power will not change her mind.

This concept may run counter to everything you have been taught and observed. You've seen men use pickup lines, money, flowers, cards, expensive dinners, clothes and Lord knows what else to impress women. All that isn't necessary. Women do enjoy the attention, but these things will not win a woman's heart. There was a point in my life when I had little money. I couldn't give a woman anything other than my time. Despite this I had more dating choices than I knew how to handle. Why? These women chose me. I didn't use pickup lines or tell them what they wanted to hear and yet they chose to go out with me. In many cases I didn't make the first move. I have had women approach me and initiate conversation. All this happened because I knew the secret: **Women choose the men.**

I remember talking with a young lady I had known for a few months. By the way, she approached me. Anyway, I was playing around by giving her a seductive look. She thought I was trying to impress her. I told her that I don't try to impress women. A man will impress (or fail to impress) a woman no matter what he does. I think one problem with a nice guy is

Rom Wills

that he tries too hard to impress a woman. He tries to show her that he is nice and responsible, how much money he has, or thousand other things. There was a man I'll call Robert, who thought he was a serious ladies' man. He would meet a woman and try to impress her with his attorney position, his membership in an upscale club in the Washington, D.C. area, and his material possessions. Robert would also ask very intimate questions about the woman's sex life. Robert rarely, if ever, got any play. Now the interesting thing is that I have never met Robert and wouldn't know him if I bumped into him on the street. I heard about Robert from women he tried to seduce. They all said the same thing about him: He turned them off. These same women have all gone out with me. Now this man was not a nice guy, but I used this example to illustrate my point. Most men try too hard to impress a woman. Many nice guys turn women off by trying to impress them. A woman will be impressed by the man of her choosing regardless of what he does for her. Never **try** to impress a woman.

Why Women Should Choose the Men

A man and woman meet in a bar. A man sees a nice beautiful face and body. He is fantasizing about how she would look naked. He isn't thinking beyond sex. The woman finds the man attractive as well. When

20

she looks at him she sees that he looks healthy and has good teeth. She checks out how he is dressed. He looks like he has a good job, which means he may be responsible. She wonders if he is the type who would fool around on her. She wonders how he will look and behave a year into the future.

The above scenario happens when women meet men. The man doesn't think beyond the bedroom. Women think about the morning and weeks after. Women think ahead. They generally exercise care in choosing a man. Even women who choose knuckleheads generally know what they are getting into. Think about it like this. Women know they can get almost any man they want for just sex. As a result of this mindset women look beyond sex when they check out a man. At least they do this when they want a man for the long term. If all they want is sex the man simply has to look good and turn them on.

Choosing a mate is an important decision. Most men are not picky enough. Most men marry the woman who was most available to them for sex. Men typically don't care about the woman's educational level, finances, or social ability. Women, on the other hand, are not moved solely by sex. Good sex yes, but that's another chapter. Therefore it isn't the only thing they consider when checking out a man. Now think about this. Who should make the initial decision about mating? The man who isn't thinking past the bedroom or the woman who is? Women instinctively know that there is more to a relationship than sexual compatibility.

RECOGNIZING THAT THE WOMAN HAS CHOSEN YOU

Now that you know women choose the men, the next step is to recognize when the woman has chosen you. This is a tricky area. Different women have different ways of catching a man's attention. It honestly takes years of observation to recognize these ways. I will provide some of the more general ways a woman will show her interest in a man. I emphasize the word **general** with regard to the following descriptions.

Smiling

The most common thing a woman may do to show her interest is to smile when she sees you. The trick here is determining in what context is she smiling. Sometimes a woman walking down the street may have the type of personality where she smiles at everybody she passes. This woman may smile at you without having the slightest romantic interest in you. On the other hand, a woman may see you and smile out of the blue. This woman obviously likes something she sees. She may even say hello. This woman is a potential date. I say potential because many women may see somebody on the street they think is attractive, smile, and then go about their business.

If you see a woman consistently at say, a bus stop, and she always smiles when she sees you, that's an excellent hint she's interested. As a rule of thumb, if a woman doesn't know your name and she smiles whenever she sees you, she is interested. Not necessarily in a romantic sense, but she does have some interest.

Her Eyes

It is said that eyes cannot lie. I have noticed one thing in my many years of dealing with different women from all over the world. If they do not like you, they will not look at you. Sounds simple? Not really. If you are on a date with a woman or you are approaching a woman or doing anything with a woman, how she looks at you will communicate her interest in you. For example, Tony approached a woman in a bookstore. He asked all sorts of questions and she answered him calmly. Tony thought the conversation went well, so he asked for her phone number. She politely told him no and left the store. Tony was hurt because he thought everything was going well. Tony should have realized she really didn't have any interest in him because during the entire conversation the woman barely looked at him. If a woman doesn't look at you she isn't interested no matter how well you think things are going.

Talking

A great sign a woman is interested in you is that she tries to talk to you. If you are walking down the street and some woman initiates conversation with you, she may be interested. Some women are aggressive about approaching the men they find attractive. Sometimes you might be bopping down the street minding your business when a woman will approach you, smile, look you dead in the eye, and ask some seemingly innocent question. If you give her an answer and she keeps talking and asking questions, generally she's interested.

Many times you may see a woman around the office, the gym, your grocery store, or the bus stop. You actually know her and she's always friendly, but you don't think she's interested. She probably is. If a woman always stops to talk with you, she has some interest. If a woman is interested in you, she will go out of her way to talk to you. She will also try to talk to you as much as possible. Keith works as a paralegal on the fourth floor of a building owned by a law firm. Karen works as a law clerk on the eleventh floor. Karen is really interested in going out with Keith. Karen, however, is not the type of woman to ask a man out. So to communicate her interest she goes out of her way to talk to Keith as much as possible. She smiles when she sees him and she always keeps her attention on him. Keith, on the hand, is totally oblivious to her actions. Karen has chosen Keith and by not recognizing this Keith is losing out on a great woman.

Touching

In my opinion, the best sign that a woman is interested in you is when she touches you. By touching I mean that she may stand real close to you when she talks or she touches your arm or shoulder. The key here is to recognize whether she is touching you because she is interested or because she is touchy when she talks to people. Some women are just touchy. If you are in a setting where you can observe the woman interacting with other people, watch how she touches them. If she doesn't touch them while talking but touches you, then she is interested in you. If she touches everybody then she might not have a romantic interest in you. One observation I have made while interacting with women over the years is that women will avoid touching or even being around a man they don't like. No matter what a woman may say, generally, if she touches, or stands close to you, she is interested in something.

Rom Wills

A Final Word About Women Choosing the Men

Women choose the men. There is nothing we can or should do to change this. Men can save a lot of time and energy by realizing this. The man, however, still plays an important role. Once a man realizes he has been chosen it is his duty to let that woman know where he stands. Women, once they choose a man, will hold out hope of getting him no matter what the circumstances. If she doesn't have a chance with him he needs to let her know so she can move on. In other words he must accept the choice. If he isn't interested he should either ignore her or let her know in the best way what his feelings are.

Categories of Men

Women, regardless of their race or class, tend to put men into two categories, select and non-select. The men in the select group are generally handsome, successful, and charismatic. These men can walk into a room full of 100 women and 70 of them will find the men attractive. These are the men women will be most receptive to. The men in the non-select group can walk into room full of 100 women and are lucky if 10 women even notice them. These men are generally invisible to women.

Jonathan is one of the select. He is handsome, has a muscular build, a high paying job, dresses stylishly, has a beautiful condo in an upscale neighborhood, and owns a late model luxury car. Jonathan knows he's the man and is conceited. When he walks into a club, women go crazy. They display their legs, breasts, or whatever they think will draw Jonathan's attention. Women even go up to Jonathan and ask him to dance. They may buy him a drink. Jonathan takes for granted he will walk out of the club with the woman of his choice.

Barry is one of the non-select. Barry is average looking on a good day. He has a slim build, average job, cheap looking clothes, shares an apartment in a working class neighborhood, and doesn't own a car. Barry is the type of man who will one day be a millionaire but doesn't act like it because of his modesty. Barry will walk into a club and women won't even glance his way. Barry will ask several women to dance and they will turn him down only to dance with another man a few minutes later. The few women who do talk to Barry want him to buy them expensive drinks. At the end of the night Barry leaves the club the same way he arrived: alone.

The key thing to remember about the select and non-select groups is that it is all based on the woman's perception. In ten years Jonathan may be overweight, without a job, and back living with his parents while Barry may be a millionaire businessman with a mansion and built like Tyson Beckford. Barry is the better man based on his personality and ambition but he doesn't have what it takes to attract women to him at first. A man has to be attractive in some way to have a woman choose him initially. Women don't have the time or energy to check out every single man they come across. Women try to determine on first look whether or not a man has it going on. At the very least, women try to determine if the man is worth getting to know. When women talk about the shortage of good men what they really mean is that there is a shortage of men in the select group.

Sub-Categories of Men

There are four general sub-categories of men in terms of how women classify them. Two of the sub-categories are in the select group while the other two sub-categories are in the non-select group. The two sub-categories in the select group are the Mr. Goodbars and the Masked Men. The two sub-categories in the non-select group are the Nice Guys and the Gamesmen. Every man fits into one of these categories or did fit at one time, as it is possible to evolve out of these categories. Each type of man represents something different to women. The man reading this should try to figure out which group he falls into. Ask any woman which group she thinks you fall into. Her answers will give you a great idea about how you are perceived by women and quite frankly may explain any problems you have experienced in relationships.

Rom Wills

Mr. Goodbar

Mr. Goodbar has it made. Women fall all over themselves to be with this man. They pay his way on dates. They give him money. Mr. Goodbar can live rent-free at a woman's apartment. They will do whatever he asks. Who is Mr. Goodbar? Mr. Goodbar is the man women read about in romance novels. Mr. Goodbar is the man who has what I call genetic beauty. Most women and even heterosexual men will look at this man and consider him handsome. This is the man with the smooth skin, sexy eyes, straight teeth, nice lips, and whatever else people consider handsome. Women get breathless when they see this man. Another type of Mr. Goodbar is a man with an average face and an exceptional physique. These men know they look good and generally dress to compliment their bodies. Another term for Mr. Goodbar is "pretty boy." Mr. Goodbar is more than a handsome face and nice body. Plenty of men are handsome with nice bodies but still don't get play. The thing that separates Mr. Goodbar from the rest is attitude. He knows how to push a woman's romantic buttons. He knows how to charm women. He knows that women choose the men and who they will choose. Mr. Goodbar knows how to make women work for his attention. Mr. Goodbar is not pressed. Jim, the prototype Mr. Goodbar said, "The best way to get a woman, especially a beautiful woman, is to ignore her. This drives them crazy. They'll want you more then. Gimme another beer."

Men like this have a tendency to become self-centered. Of the four groups, Mr. Goodbar works the least to keep a relationship going. They don't have to. If one woman doesn't like how the relationship is progressing, Mr. Goodbar simply moves on to the next woman. The only time Mr. Goodbar is alone is when he wants to be. This is the man women want the most. When you read articles in women's magazines about how they want a man to be kind and sensitive, they really want Mr. Goodbar to read the articles and become kind and sensitive. Many women will trample 10 nice guys to get to one Mr. Goodbar. Some women will even marry a nice guy and keep a Mr. Goodbar on the side.

Cedrick is a Mr. Goodbar. He is quite aware of the power he has over women. Cedrick is handsome, tall, and works as a model. He is always the most stylish man in the room, even at the grocery store. Even though Cedrick makes more than enough money he rarely pays for dates. Cedrick rarely approaches women. They usually approach him. Cedrick has slept with so many women that one day he met a woman he slept with years in the past and introduced himself as if he just met her. Cedrick keeps women on edge because they realize he can dismiss them at a moment's notice. Cedrick seems to have it made. That is not the case.

Despite the number of women Cedrick has chasing him there is one woman he wants above all others. Cedrick is in love with Denise but it is an unrequited love. Denise thinks Cedrick is handsome and sexy but she isn't interested in Cedrick beyond friendship. Denise wants a handsome and sexy man but also someone with spiritual values. Denise wants a man with a certain sense of responsibility, ambition, and honesty. Denise is beautiful and carries herself with respect. Cedrick would drop every other woman and be a one-woman man if Denise would have him.

Mr. Goodbar is the man who attracts most of the women and is the envy of most other men. Mr. Goodbar, however, doesn't always end up with the woman he wants.

The Masked Man

The Masked Man is the man who doesn't have the raw sex appeal of Mr. Goodbar. He is average looking to most women, handsome to a few. The Masked Man may have to spend more time working on his looks. Whereas Mr. Goodbar can get away with not shaving for a few days and miss trips to the barbershop, the Masked Man must make more of an effort at grooming. Of the four groups the Masked Man will make himself attractive. The Masked Man makes up for what he lacks in looks with impeccable grooming and a dynamic personal style. The Masked Man is typically successful. The man gets paid. He has a certain status that is respected in society. He has the car and the house. He's invited to all the happening parties. The Masked Man has enough going for him that women will try to get to know him even if they are not physically attracted to him.

The Masked Man will, however, have some issues. He typically had to work hard to get to the point where women find him desirable. He had to put in long hours in school and on the job. He had to live paycheck to paycheck for a long time. The Masked Man may have had many painful relationship experiences. He may have been ignored because he was unattractive. He might not have got the time of day because he didn't look successful. The Masked Man may wear the mask of success but under the mask he has battle scars. Getting to the top is a fight and staying there is a harder fight. This has a big effect on their relationships with women. Many Masked Men didn't have the support of women outside of their mother or sisters in their struggle for success. As a result these men may not be in a big hurry to settle down.

Women in high school and college ignored Lonnie. He didn't date until after college and he didn't lose his virginity until he was 26. Lonnie was average-

Rom Wills

looking with crooked teeth and 50 pounds overweight. He didn't dress well. Lonnie, however, was good with computers. He could write programs for anything. After working for a computer company for a couple of years, Lonnie followed his dream and started his own company. It was tough going at first. He had to live with his mother and work out of her basement for the first few years. He didn't have a car during this time. He didn't have a steady girlfriend despite being kind and ambitious. After the first few years Lonnie's business began to pick up. As Lonnie got more money he was able to buy a house and a nice car. Lonnie also joined a gym and got braces. He began to take better care of himself and as a result began to look better. As he became more and more successful and well known the same women who had ignored him in high school and college began to see him as attractive. The same women who called him fat and ugly now began to tell him how they always liked him and thought he would make something out of his life. Lonnie laughed at these women. He couldn't take them seriously. Lonnie had been alone for so long that all he wanted from a woman was sex. Even then the woman had to be superfine. Lonnie began to dog women. He couldn't let go of his past pain despite his success. A woman seeing past the mask would not recognize the man underneath.

The Masked Man may want someone special

but until he can let go of his pain he will likely avoid serious relationships.

The Nice Guy

Everybody knows about the Nice Guy. He is polite, dependable, hardworking, and believes in putting a woman on a pedestal. He never plays games with women. He believes in being loyal. His woman never has to worry about where he is. He cooks for her and is always trying to be romantic. He is thoughtful. Outside of what he does for her he is active in the community. He is active in church and is a big brother to fatherless boys. He would seem like the man women would be all over to marry. As we all know this is not the case.

The Nice Guy doesn't move women in a romantic way. He is dependable and responsible but all too often the Nice Guy finds out that these are not the traits that attract women to men. The Nice Guy typically has average looks and dresses in an average way or in some cases not well at all. He doesn't have a body that stands out in a crowd. The Nice Guy lacks personal magnetism. The Nice Guy, despite his shortcomings, tries hard with women. He will meet a beautiful woman and do everything for her to show how nice he is. He does things for her, gives her money and waits for her to be ready for sex no matter how much he wants her. The women who give him the time of day usually take advantage of the Nice Guy's generosity. Since he is not the most handsome or charismatic, the Nice Guy is usually ignored.

Dejuan is a Nice Guy. He is kind, polite, mature, and responsible. He is short with a slim build and a head big for his body. He dresses in clothes that are comfortable for him, but are not in step with the current fashions. He lives with his parents because he cannot afford his own place. He works as an office clerk at a law firm. He believes in community service and is active with his church. People who meet him consider him to be a good person. Many people believe that one day he will make a good husband for some lucky lady. Ladies, on the other hand, do not think so.

When Dejuan meets women they dismiss him or see him as a buddy who they can hang out with while they wait for Mr. Right. When women have shown romantic interest, Dejuan would discover that they were trying to get what little bit of money he had. The only time Dejuan has had sex was when a friend might have felt some sympathy for him. Women generally cry on his shoulders about the men who dogged them. Often the women would complain about the shortage of good men right in his presence. Dejuan cannot understand why a woman will say she wants a good man and look right past him.

The Nice Guy has to get to the point where

women stop looking past him.

The Gamesman

The Gamesman is average looking, has an average job if he is even working, and has typically been burned in his many dealings with the opposite sex. He realizes that he doesn't have the tools to succeed with the woman of the new millennium. He typically doesn't have the looks or the money. His only options are to withdraw from the game or pretend he is one of the select. The Gamesman is the Nice Guy who has decided that enough is enough. The Gamesman is the man who lies, cheats, and does whatever it takes to bed women. He is ruthless. He is the type of man who will dog a woman out whenever the opportunity presents itself. He is all about getting his.

The Gamesman presents an illusion to women. He reads the articles and the books. He tries to look and act like the man women want but he lacks the substance. The Gamesman uses every ploy in his arsenal. He acts like a devout Christian for the church going lady. He is a business owner for a high-powered attorney. He borrows his friend's car to impress a young lady. He pretends his friend's hi-rise condo is his own. He will have phony business cards printed up. I heard of one Gamesman who went as far as to get a phony listing in a phone directory. The Gamesman succeeds until women begin to see through his game. Some women see through the game from the get-go and decide to play along. Very often his own games burn the Gamesman.

Evan is a Gamesman. For the time being he is house sitting at a condo for a friend. Evan has a sporadic employment history. Presently he is unemployed. Evan is average looking but is a stylish dresser. When he does work he spends his money on clothes. Evan also works out consistently so he has a pretty decent build. Evan gets plenty of attention from the ladies because he drives his friend's Porsche. Evan goes to clubs during happy hour and buys drinks at half-price and passes out business cards identifying him as the president of an export business. Occasionally, he will bring a woman back to his friend's condo and act like the place is his. This plan works for a couple of months while his friend is out of town. When the friend comes back into town Evan is forced to come up with different stories to explain why he isn't at his condo. Eventually Evan will be forced to start a new game with a different set of women.

Gamesmen have an idea of the tools necessary to succeed with women but they don't try to develop them.

The Real Man

The above four categories correspond loosely to terms described by Yao Nyamekye Morris in his book, ***The Yao of Holistic Living***. My interpretations are based on my personal observations of the groups initially outlined by Mr. Morris. Other people may have different interpretations. To these categories I will add a fifth: The Real Man. He may or may not be physically handsome. Women who meet him consider him to be attractive regardless of his physical features. He dresses to compliment his body. He keeps himself in good physical shape. He is hardworking with plans for the future. He treats women with the utmost respect. He doesn't however, allow women to run over him. Despite being attractive to several women he is waiting for his soulmate. He doesn't bother with women unless they can have a positive influence on his life. He doesn't play games and is honest with himself and with others. The Real Man knows who he is and where he is going.

The Real Man has flaws like everybody else. The difference is that he acknowledges his flaws. He is not perfect but he takes full responsibility for his actions. When he says he's going to do something he does it. He can handle his business. The Real Man can satisfy a woman intellectually, emotionally, and physically. When women talk about Mr. Right they are talking about the Real Man.

Kirk is a Real Man who used to be a Mr. Goodbar. All he used to do was hang out, play ball, and get into trouble. Kirk is tall with a muscular body. When he was a Mr. Goodbar, Kirk kept up with the latest fashions. He used to sell drugs to finance his lifestyle. He had it all: cars, women, and a reputation. A brush with death, however, changed Kirk's perspective on life. Kirk began to read more. He mainly read non-fiction books, which raised his consciousness. Kirk began to think about his actions towards himself and others. He began to think about the future. Kirk started writing short stories and poems about his experiences. He began to treat women better. Eventually he met a beautiful woman he was able to completely satisfy and she was able to compliment him. Kirk is happy for the first time in his life.

Will is a Real Man. For years Will was a Nice Guy. He would do anything for women. Will was overweight and average height. He never did anything to make himself more physically attractive. He made a decent salary, which he spent recklessly in trying to win affection from women. Women would take his money and his time but never gave him anything in return. Finally, Will had enough. He decided to change his life. Will read books on relationships and began to ask different women questions about what they wanted in a man. Will then developed a program to improve himself. First he joined a gym to work on his body. He talked with his friends about how to dress better. He became more assertive. He began demanding, and getting, respect from women. Will was still kind but he was not a pushover. Will became more attractive to women. He was now muscular, confident, and a good dresser. With these traits added to his intelligence and sensitivity, Will became quite a catch. Will didn't let it go to his head. Despite the new attention from women, Will is saving his love for one special lady.

The Real Man is the one the ladies want. Women need to be satisfied on all levels. They have to be attracted to a man physically, intellectually, emotionally, and spiritually. Mr. Goodbar, the Masked Man, the Nice Guy, and the Gamesman cannot fully satisfy the needs of women. For this reason, many women have two or more men. Charlotte is married to a wonderful man, Stephan. He is responsible and works hard to provide for his wife. Stephan, however, isn't very attractive or good in bed. For that reason Charlotte has been having a long running affair with a young man on her job. Many women do this. Charlotte would prefer a man who can satisfy her completely. All women and men want somebody who can meet all our needs. Unfortunately, most people can only satisfy some of their partner's needs.

An Understanding of Women

Women mystify most men. Even men who get lots of dates are mystified. Women do things and view life differently from men. Their different viewpoints often cause conflicts with the men in their lives. Many men don't understand women or even take the time to understand women. The men who take the time to understand women get plenty of play. A man must develop an understanding of women and their thought processes. As I explained previously women choose the men and there are select and non-select groups of men. How a woman selects a man is based on her particular needs. A woman working on a minimum wage job and living in a poor neighborhood may look for a man with money. A woman with a high-powered job and a four-bedroom house may look for a man who is sexually appealing since she doesn't really need anything else from him. A man should keep this in perspective. Often a man will wonder why a particular woman is not interested in him despite what he has going for him. Ted wonders why Wanda barely pays attention to him. Ted has a slamming job, is well educated, and has a house and car. Most women consider Ted handsome. Wanda, however, isn't attracted to Ted because she believes a relationship with him would be too tame. Wanda is a drama queen and Ted is a no-nonsense man. He has to realize that he doesn't fit her needs. I have observed several factors which influences a woman's decision to choose a particular man. The major factors are vanity, insecurity, excitement, and a need to nurture.

Vanity

Women are vain. They want attention. If you encounter a woman who tries to tell you otherwise, she's lying. You see proof of their vanity every day. Look at the cosmetics industry. Women will spend hours fixing their hair and putting on makeup. Why? To look attractive. Why do they want to look nice? They are vain. Women want attention from men. I remember a time I was in downtown Washington, D.C. when I noticed a nice looking woman walking through a group of bike messengers. They were saying all sorts of vulgar things to her, yet she walked through ignoring their comments. I felt bad for her until I saw where she was going. She was going to her car and I noticed that she could have easily avoided walking through the messengers. She wanted their attention. Women will wear provocative clothing and then act like they are mad when someone makes a crude comment. If a woman doesn't want to attract crude comments, she knows how to avoid this situation. A woman knows that high heels, silk stockings, and a mini-skirt will attract men. She wears this because she wants to attract attention and this makes her feel good about herself. A woman wants to feel desirable.

A woman's vanity is a big factor in why women fall in love with men who are bad for them. Janet is a short chubby woman with adult acne. Most men find her unattractive. She can go to a club, ask a man to dance and get rejected. Janet has a nice apartment, extra money, and a car. One day while shopping she meets Mark. Mark is fairly handsome and a smooth talker, a Gamesman. Mark approaches her in the store and starts a conversation. He calls her very attractive and asks for her phone number. They go out that night and Janet has the time of her life. Mark makes Janet feel like a queen. They make love that night. They spend a lot of time together those first few weeks. During this time Mark gradually moves clothes into Janet's apartment until they are living together. Janet is happier than she has ever been. She falls in love. That's when things begin to change. Mark begins to sneak around on Janet. He becomes emotionally and physically abusive. He starts taking her for granted. Janet will hold on to him anyway. Why? Mark made her feel good. He played to her vanity. Janet wanted someone to give her attention and by doing so Mark was able to take advantage of her. Women in most cases get hooked on players because these men played to their vanity.

Playing to a woman's vanity works for any man. A nice guy reading this probably will not take advantage of a woman. You can still keep her attention after she has chosen you by complimenting her, telling her she looks beautiful, and smells good. By the same token, you can play to a woman's vanity by not complimenting her. Ned attracts several women not because he compliments them, but because he ignores them. Ned is nerd trapped in model's body. Ned would rather spend time in a library than in a club. Women who encounter Ned all but hit him on the head to get his attention. If a woman has chosen you and either you don't recognize this or choose to ignore her she will work to get your attention. Look at it another way. Have you been in or seen a situation where a man does everything to win a woman's affections only to be rejected? Now if the man accepts the rejection and moves on many times the woman will begin showing more interest in the man. Why? She enjoyed the attention. She doesn't want it to stop. As long as you are able to play to women's vanity, you will always have dates. Look at it yet another way. When a woman strokes your ego it certainly makes you feel good doesn't it? Everyone wants to feel special and attractive.

Insecurity

Many women are insecure. This insecurity affects how a woman chooses a man. Stephanie is insecure about her looks. As a result she avoids men she considers too handsome. She chooses men who are ugly because she will always look better. Gina is insecure about her financial status. She always chooses men who are financially secure. Paula is insecure about her desirability to men. She will do anything to keep a man. In some poor areas a woman may choose a man renowned for his ability to fight. The reason is that he can physically protect her. All of these women chose men who provided them with a sense of security. This security can be emotional, physical, financial, anything according to the woman's needs.

Despite what you might see, most women are insecure and not confident about many things. A woman will be insecure about her looks, her body, her viewpoints, and a countless variety of things. They will worry about things that a man could care less about. Most men don't worry if they are too fat, too short, or if their hair looks just right. If we do worry, we usually do something about it. Most men don't worry about being considered handsome. Men accept themselves more. Annette is an extremely beautiful woman. Men see her and fall in love with her instantly. Annette on the other hand thinks she is ugly. She doesn't think she has an attractive body part. As a result of her insecurity she never believes that men actually find her attractive. She stays lonely as a result. Insecurity causes many women to not believe in themselves. Deep down they may not believe they are good enough to attract men. This is one reason why women respond to confident and aggressive men. These men believe in themselves and in their ability to face life. I will talk more about confident and aggressive men later.

Many men, particularly nice guys, appear to be wimpy in women's eyes. How is a woman going to feel secure if she's with a man she thinks is too wimpy to take charge? Many nice guys worship the women they are with. Nice guys allow the woman to run the relationship. An insecure woman will feel even more insecure with a man she can boss around. Women, regardless of their place in life, want a man who is secure and has the ability to make her feel secure. Joy has a high-paying job, and a big house but doesn't have a man in her life. She has high standards. She wants a man who has more than her. She is not a gold digger. She already has money. Joy wants a man with more because despite her success she still has some insecurities. She wants a man who can provide her with security.

The bottom line is that a woman will always be attracted to a man who can provide security. A tall woman wants a taller man. A woman with a college degree wants a man with a graduate degree. Someone making $50,000 will want someone making $60,000. For any relationship to work the woman must always look up to the man with respect. It may sound sexist but I challenge you to find a male/female relationship that is harmonious with the woman being in a superior position. You won't find it. When I say a superior position I am speaking in terms of a woman feeling like her man cannot alleviate her insecurities. Christina makes more money than Cory. She has a nicer apartment and car. Christina still feels secure with Cory because he is ambitious and is always working to better himself. On another level he doesn't allow anyone to disrespect her.

One thing men really need to understand is that it's a scary world out there for women. Many women have to face loneliness, raising children without a man, underemployment, and worst of all, they constantly have to be on guard against physical attacks the most common of which is rape. Women need and want men who will protect them and make life easier. Ladies are not asking for perfection. They simply want a man who can make them feel secure.

Excitement

Women want excitement. One of the biggest complaints women have is that too many men are dull. Most women live dull enough lives. They do not need a dull man to make matters worse. Jackie works a 9 to 5 job as an administrative assistant. She does the same thing every day. Along comes Edgar. Edgar is spontaneous. He works as a private investigator so he always has an exciting story to tell. He works his own hours so he can always surprise Jackie with lunch. When they go out their dates are always memorable. Their relationship is never routine. Edgar provides Jackie with excitement she would never have otherwise.

Think back to what I said about a woman's insecurity. This insecurity prevents many women from doing anything exciting on their own. Women generally don't take risks. Women more so than men play it safe. Playing it safe is boring some times. Women want excitement. That's one reason why romance novels are so popular. If you ever get the chance, go to a bookstore and read the back of a romance novel. Even buy one. Say you are getting a gift for your sister if you're embarrassed. These novels never have dull men. The men are always exciting with a certain edge to them. Women want that feeling of excitement when they deal with a man. Too many men often play it safe because it seems more responsible and they think that's what women want. Women want both responsibility and excitement. Take Edgar. He is spontaneous yet he takes his job responsibilities seriously. It is possible to be both.

This sense of excitement is why many women fall for players. If nothing else, players provide excitement. A nice guy is seen as someone who is responsible, does the right things, and plays it safe. They are especially seen as dull. I know several nice guys who are anything but dull. My view, however, doesn't matter. Women make the choice. Women go for the men they think are exciting.

Need to Nurture

Women have a strong need to nurture the people in their lives. This is part of their nature and their special beauty. Some men would be lost if some woman didn't love them enough to take care of them. Often you hear women talk about molding a man or in harsher terms, "training" him. There was a time when I was greatly offended by this notion. As my experience and insight grew I realized women don't try to mold men because of some nefarious plot. It is simply their nature. For that reason a woman may skip over a man who looks like he has his act together and get involved with Joe Ruffneck who she believes needs a little push to get going in life. Many women get played because of this but that need to nurture is still there. Anya is the type of woman who goes for the nerdiest looking men. She tries to get them to dress better and be more assertive. She has an idea of what she wants in a man and she believes if she shows a man enough love he'll become her ideal.

Crystal is the type of woman willing to listen to the problems of her male friends. She is supportive of their efforts and many of her friends have gone on to become successful. The most appreciative man is Sam. Crystal supported him when he had nothing. She never gave him money. Her support was emotional. That support, however, helped Sam to succeed with a risky business venture. Sam and Crystal are now married.

Despite what many men think and believe, most women are supportive of men going in a positive direction. There are some who are not supportive but they are in the minority and quite frankly are not worth the time it takes to think about them. Women want their men to rise as high as the sun. When men do rise we have to remember to bring the women who supported us on our journey. It was their love that helped get us to that point. Women really want to feel like they have made a difference in their men's lives. If you come off like you don't need a woman they will leave you alone. This doesn't mean she wants to be your mother, she just wants to make a difference.

What It All Boils Down To

Women are vain, insecure, seek excitement, and have a need to nurture. Ultimately, what it boils down to is that women choose men according to their needs. If a woman needs a man who is going to give her attention he is the type of man she will choose. An insecure woman chooses a man who can make her feel secure. Women seeking excitement look for men who can provide it. Nurturing women find men they can nurture. Women don't choose men simply because they look good or are confident or aggressive. They choose men because of some need that has to be satisfied. Needs dictate desires. Women will always choose men according to their needs.

Attractive Traits

You know that women choose the men. You realize men must recognize when they have been chosen. Now I'll tell you about what factors attract a woman to a man. These factors are both mental and physical. I have had conversations with more than a thousand women on the subject. I made my own observations from personal experiences. Finally, over the years I have had conversations with and observed all types of men from the biggest nerd to the most prolific womanizers. These men and women have had a wide variety of opinions on the dynamics of male/ female relationships. After listening to all these people, reading books, and examining my own personal experiences, I realized the reasons why some men get all the women and some men do not get the time of day. There are certain personality and physical traits women gravitate toward regardless of race or background. I will now share these traits with you.

PERSONALITY TRAITS

Confidence

Women are attracted to confident men. This confidence may be manifested in different ways. With one man it may be how he speaks. Another man may show confidence in the way he walks. Yet another man may show confidence in taking charge of a bad situation. Confidence is a key to attracting women. Looks and money are nowhere near as important as confidence.

A nice guy constantly wonders why he's alone at night while a player will have more women than he can handle. John is hardworking, polite, and responsible. He met a young lady named Emily at his gym. Emily found John attractive, so she was interested in getting to know him better. John thought the same of Emily and communicated this interest to some friends at the gym. John would talk to Emily, but would never ask her out. Her beauty intimidated him and he was afraid of rejection. He was afraid even if they did go out he couldn't show her a good time. John was worried about satisfying her if they had sex. John decided not to ask her out. What John didn't know was Emily knew how he felt about her. After several weeks of dropping hints, Emily decided she was not interested in John for anything beyond friendship.

Donald joined the gym a few weeks later. His first night he saw Emily and approached her because she smiled at him. Donald wasn't as physically attractive as John, but he moved about in a confident manner. Donald approached Emily, talked with her for a little while and then invited her out for drinks. Donald and Emily became a steady couple afterwards. Donald got the girl, not only because he picked up on Emily's interest in him, but also because he was confident.

Confidence is nothing more than belief in yourself. Many men don't believe in their ability to attract a woman. Many men don't show confidence in how they carry themselves. They never assert themselves in a situation because they don't believe it would be "nice" to do so. They are not confident of their ability to take charge in a relationship. They'll let the woman make the decisions for the relationship. Sadly, many men try to be so nice and accommodating to others that they are afraid to be themselves. They don't have confidence in their own personalities. The most important personality factor that separates the nice guy who doesn't receive attention from the player who does is confidence.

Aggressiveness

Women are attracted to men who have aggressive natures. I don't mean aggressive as in someone who bullies and beats up people. I mean aggressive in terms of taking the initiative. Using the example of John, Emily, and Donald again, Donald hooked up with Emily because he recognized she was interested and acted on that observation. Even though women choose the men, men still have to recognize when they've been chosen. Women want a man who knows what he wants and is willing to get it. They don't want a wimp. Eddie and Frank are trying to win the affection of Sheila. Sheila is casually dating both men and she wants to settle with just one. When Eddie and Sheila plan dates, Sheila makes most of the decisions. Sheila decides whether they should go to dinner or the movies. She orders from the menu for both of them. She offers to pay Dutch and Eddie lets her. Eddie has no problems letting Sheila make the primary decisions during their dates.

Frank on the other hand, is always making the dating decisions. He tells Sheila where they will be going on the date. He picks her up, orders for both of them, pays for everything, and afterwards may do something spontaneous. Frank always takes charge of a situation. For that reason Sheila chooses to go out with Frank exclusively.

The above example may seem extreme. I used it to illustrate my point. Women respond to aggressive men. This aggressiveness extends beyond dating. A man aggressive in his daily life always attracts more women than a passive man. Patrick is aggressive in how he goes through life. He is aggressive about getting on the bus first. He is aggressive about presenting his ideas on different work projects. Patrick aggressively expresses his views on any and all subjects. Women are all over Patrick and he aggressively pursues the women of his choosing. These women are attracted to his aggressiveness.

Women want confident and aggressive men in their lives. A woman wants a man who can look her square in the eye and say, "Baby, I can handle this." They want a man who is going to actively pursue a living and one who will provide for their needs. Even the most nurturing woman doesn't want a weak man. How is a woman supposed to feel secure with this type of man? A woman doesn't want to hear her man say he can't get a job or that he was passed over for a promotion because he was too afraid to ask for one. Passiveness doesn't keep the rent paid. Passiveness doesn't feed the children. A man's woman and children do not, I repeat, **DO NOT,** want to hear that their needs are not being met because of a hostile society, "the man" or whatever. They want to know the rent is paid and food is on the table. A starving belly does not hear any excuses. **WOMEN WANT MEN WHO CAN HANDLE THEIR BUSINESS!!!** The man who is confident and aggressive has the ability to handle his business.

PHYSICAL APPEARANCE

Introduction

I constantly read in magazines about how women choose men solely because of their personalities. Surveys and interviews always indicate women are less concerned with physical appearance than men. I only have one thing to say about this: **Stop the Madness!** A woman will indeed choose a man because of personality but it is his appearance that attracts her in the first place. Gillian checks out men all the time. She looks at their physiques, hair, grooming, clothes, shoes, everything external. Women are exactly like men as far as appearance is concerned, probably worse. If a woman doesn't like something about a man's physical appearance, she will either leave him alone or try to make changes. Look at it this way. Steven is confident and aggressive and yet he still doesn't get any play. You're probably saying that according to "Nice Guys and Players" Steven should be making out like a bandit. The problem with Steven is he has a bad haircut, thick glasses, yellow crooked teeth, skinny body with a potbelly, and he smells. On top of that his clothes are dirty and ill kempt. I have observed women turning up their noses at men who look like this. Steven may be a good man but women won't be interested in finding out. Physical appearance is of paramount importance.

Face

Good news for men who don't have movie star looks. A man's face is probably the least important feature women look at when choosing a man. Winston has an ugly face. His own mother thinks so. Yet Winston gets women like crazy. Why? Winston's other attributes more than make up for not being handsome. I spoke with several women on the subject. Many women will go out with an ugly man as long as he has other things going for him. Some women even prefer ugly men. Women do like and go crazy over handsome men but they look for other factors such as confidence. Also, some women get insecure around extremely handsome men, especially if they are not as attractive. Don't think being ugly will stop women from being interested in you.

Ugly men still need to keep their face in the best

shape possible. This includes regular haircuts, great dental hygiene, and a clean face. If you are man who has been called ugly don't worry. You can't change your bone structure so you need to accept your appearance. Just find humor in your face. Jim, the patron saint of Mr. Goodbars, said, "A beautiful woman will always like an ugly man because she doesn't want to be around someone who looks better than her. Let's go buy another six-pack." No matter what your face looks like you can still attract women as long as you have confidence and other positive attributes.

Physique

Women crack me up because they try to act like they don't check out men's bodies the same way men check out women's bodies. Women are worse in that regard. If a woman isn't turned on by a man's body all the money, power, prestige, and confidence in the world won't help. You ever wonder why some men seem to get women without trying while others barely get the time of day? Look at the men who get the most women. Typically they have superior builds. They tend to have well-developed torsos. If you have trouble attracting women take a look in the mirror. If your stomach extends further out than your chest, you won't attract many women. If you have a big chest and flat stomach you will literally have your pick of women. Women are turned on by fit bodies. I've observed that having a nice body means that you don't have to spend as much money or play games. Women tend to cut to the chase when they see a man with a nice body.

Every man, single or in a relationship, should keep his body in the best shape possible. The best shape possible doesn't mean working out until you look like a bodybuilder. Quite frankly, many really muscular men are blessed with good genes or are on steroids. Best shape possible simply means the best for you. A naturally big man shouldn't aspire to look like a string bean. A naturally skinny man shouldn't aspire to look like a middle linebacker. Establish a consistent exercise routine. You look better for women and it's healthy.

Never underestimate what a good physique can do for you. Ronald was interested in Erica for years. She never saw him as anything other than a friend. Ronald had a lot going for him. Even Erica thought he was a good man, just not for her. Ronald, however, was fifty pounds overweight. Erica moved away to another city for her job. During this time Ronald started working out. The pounds melted away. After a year Erica came back to town, saw Ronald, and was immediately turned on. Ronald had gone from being a chubby soft looking fellow to a muscular hardbody.

Rom Wills

Erica suddenly found Ronald sexy. Erica became willing to do anything to win Ronald's affection. Of course, she had plenty of competition. Ronald, by starting an exercise program, went from being almost ignored by women to having his choice. Develop your physique!

Grooming

You can be built like Adonis and still not get any play. Having all the muscles in the world won't help you if you have bad breath and body odor. Grooming is of extreme importance. Many men lose out simply because they don't practice good hygiene. Look at it like this. Most men wouldn't want to go out with a dirty looking woman. Somebody may say, "This is common sense." Trust me, it's not. On countless occasions I have observed the dirtiest looking men try to pick up women in different places. They never succeed. Always keep yourself well groomed.

Clothes

There is a saying about clothes making the man. At one time I didn't believe that statement. As I got older and more experienced, I realized that statement has some validity. You can tell a lot about a man by the clothes he wears. Many women choose a man based on how he dresses. It sounds shallow but it's reality. To attract women a man should wear clothes that fit well and compliment his body. There are several ways men wear their clothes these days. I see many men wearing baggy clothes with some designer's name. I see others wearing cheap looking suits. I can always look at a group of men and tell who will get the most play. The clothes you wear and how they are worn are important.

When choosing clothes always pick the best quality. This doesn't necessarily mean some designer label. Choose quality because it lasts longer and looks better over time. Always dress neatly. Iron your shirts and put a sharp crease in your dress pants. Always keep your shoes shined. In college I probably didn't dress like your typical college student. I always wore an ironed shirt and creased pants. I was notorious for keeping my shoes shined. I didn't think women actually paid attention to how I dressed until a woman I went to school with mentioned how she liked how I kept my shirts and pants ironed and shoes shined. Just keeping your clothes neat and clean does wonders for attracting women.

Dressing classy works best in attracting women. Marcus and Rodney were buddies hanging out at a club. Marcus wore a nice dark conservative suit, white shirt, great necktie, and shined shoes. Rodney wore a tight suit, dingy shirt, cheap necktie, and worn out shoes. Marcus had several women approach him. Rodney approached several women who rejected him. The women responded to Marcus because he had on nice clothes. They weren't necessarily expensive clothes, but they looked nice on Marcus. Dressing nicely will always attract women.

One final word on clothing: Take care of your shoes. If you can only afford to go for quality in one area of your wardrobe then go for it on shoes. Women may ignore cheap clothes but they won't ignore shoes. A shoeshine kit should have an honored place in every man's home. When you shop for shoes you should search the same way you do for cars. They cost about the same anyway. Keep good shoes on your feet and you will keep women at your side.

The Bottom Line

A man must be confident, aggressive, and keep up his physical appearance. Too many men don't do anything to improve themselves. Too many men get to a point where they are comfortable and feel no need to go further. These same men wonder why women are not interested in them. They get an attitude and then blame the women for not finding them attractive. Leroy is insecure, passive, out of shape and sloppy. He thinks women have problems because they don't give him the time of day. He never once thought to change himself to become the type of man they want. Before putting women down a man needs to work on himself to become the best person he can be.

Rules For Meeting Beautiful Women

Despite knowing women choose the men, men are expected to recognize they have been chosen and make the first move. Also, you may walk down the street and see a beautiful woman on the other side. She might choose you if she sees you but you still need to make the move. After you have developed your confidence, aggressiveness, and improved your personal appearance, you still need to know how to meet beautiful women. The following are rules a man should follow in order to meet this type of woman.

Rules For Meeting Beautiful Women

Never believe a beautiful woman is beyond your reach

Remember this rule above all else. Remember what I said about confidence. Most men psych themselves out of approaching a beautiful woman. Many psych themselves out of asking a beautiful woman they already know on a date. Always **believe** you can meet and date any beautiful woman you encounter. You won't be successful all the time, but you will be most of the time. As long as you have the right frame of mind you can take comfort in knowing if you are not successful with woman A, women B and C will respond.

When you see a beautiful woman, walk up and introduce yourself

Sounds easy? For most men it's not. Most men are worried about rejection, or looking stupid or a bunch of little things too numerous to mention. Why worry? If you approach a woman, the <u>worst</u> she can do is ignore you. If she does, just walk away quietly. Her rejection won't kill you. Anyway, 99 percent of the time if you speak to a woman she will respond if you introduce yourself politely. I've had numerous women tell me they liked how I approached them and how they wished men would kindly introduce themselves. The introduction is important. No one, I repeat, no one, has gone wrong by simply saying, "Hello, my name is So and So." You may not get a phone number or even a response. Then again you might have just met your future wife. The main thing is taking that first step as opposed to sitting back wishing you could talk to that woman.

Don't be a jerk

Walking up to a woman saying something like, "Hey baby! You're phat to death!" is not going to cut it. It may work with a woman who doesn't have more respect for herself, but it won't work for the majority of women. Never be a jerk with someone you've just met. Always follow the second rule. Don't talk to the woman as if you have known her for a year. Women really do want gentlemen. I have already explained why women end up with jerks.

Don't be intimidating

When you introduce yourself don't stand in a position where you are touching the woman. The only initial contact should consist of a businesslike handshake. If further closeness develops that's all right if the woman initiates the action. The main thing a man wants to do when he meets a woman is make her feel comfortable. You are not making her feel comfortable if you are pushing up on her the first meeting. In this day and age women have to be careful. Pay attention to see if she is even interested. Is she looking you in the eye? Is she smiling? Is she touchy? With all the stalkers and rapists out there, a woman with any sense is going to be on guard. Remember what I said about insecurity. Try not to intimidate her.

Asking her for her phone number

This is an interesting area. Generally there is only one absolute rule one should follow when asking a woman for her phone number. Ask for the number when you are reasonably sure you won't see the woman again. Even then ask for a number you can reach her at, not necessarily her home number. She still might not be comfortable enough to give you her home phone number. She may be more comfortable giving you her work phone number or just taking your phone number. Observe to see if she is showing an interest. If she isn't showing an interest don't ask for her number.

If you feel you will see the woman again on a consistent basis wait a while before asking her for her number. By waiting you are more likely to get the number and much more. She has had time to get to know you.

One thing that must be stressed with this rule is

that it's the most flexible. You must judge when it is appropriate to ask a woman for her phone number. Remember, the only time a man should ask a woman for her phone number after the initial introduction should be when he is reasonably sure that he will not see the woman again.

When you get the phone number call her right away

This rule should speak for itself. Some men try to be too cool and not call the woman right away. Sometimes this actually works, depending on how pressed the woman is for you. As a general rule, call the woman right away. If not right away, tell her when you are going to call her, then call at that time. Women want men to call them. I have known several women who have suffered anxiety because a man didn't call them. I seriously believe one of the things that got me the most dates was simply calling women promptly. That one little phone call opens up so many doors. I have had women tell me they were excited when I first called them. When you get a woman's phone number, use it. Forget trying to be "too cool." Many "cool" men don't date often.

Rules For Meeting Beautiful Women
MEETING WOMEN IN DIFFERENT PLACES

Public places

Meeting a woman in a public place is tough. After all, a woman walking down the street may not be inclined to talk to you, especially if she is beautiful. Beautiful women have men trying to talk to them all day, mostly in a rude manner. For the most part, let these women go on about their business. These women are probably nice, but constant contact with men making crude suggestions may force them to act distant.

On the other hand, a beautiful woman on the street may strike you as "the one." If that's the case, you have to talk to her. As long as you apply the rules in this situation you have nothing to lose by talking to the woman. Only approach a woman on the street if you are extremely attracted to her. Also be receptive if the woman approaches you.

Another public place you may meet a beautiful woman is a store. The woman may be shopping or a store employee. If she is shopping, she may or may not be receptive. If she is browsing, she will likely talk to you, especially if it seems like you are looking for the same item. This is a great way to get a conversation started. A woman may not be receptive if she came for a specific item and is in a hurry to leave. She may not be interested in talking to anyone. You will have to judge the situation for yourself. Now a store employee may be more difficult to approach. Not because she will reject you, in most cases her job depends on showing some degree of friendliness. A beautiful woman in this case ordinarily has several men trying to talk to her daily. If the woman is appealing, I recommend taking it slow with her. Observe to see if she is showing an interest. An example would be walking up to ask her about some item and nothing more. Don't go any further unless there is a golden opportunity or she initiates the conversation. Otherwise, after she helps you go on about your business. Afterwards go back to the store a couple more times to get her used to seeing you. At that point follow the rules and you are home free.

A great public place to meet a beautiful woman is at a bus stop or train station. Using myself as an example, I have dated several women whom I have met at subway stations or bus stops. It's the same situation every time. I would see a woman at a certain time on my way to or from work. After seeing her a few times I usually walked up to her, introduced myself, said something like, "I always see you here. My name is Rom." Worked every time. Once I have done this I talk to them on a consistent basis, usually going out with them a month or so later. Since I knew where they were going to be at a given time I had time to get to know them and have them feel comfortable around me.

Clubs/Parties

Meeting beautiful women at clubs can be easy and difficult. Easy because in most cases the women are at the club to meet somebody. Difficult because they may be looking for a specific type of man. At clubs women look for men who look, dance, and talk a certain way along with a willingness to pay for drinks. If you don't fit this bill give it up. If you do, it's like a turkey shoot. Despite this, at clubs I have constantly observed men standing around like they are afraid to approach a beautiful woman. This is stupid. A woman **will not** dress up in a tight sexy dress, silk stockings, pumps, have her hair and face done, and wear expensive perfume, if she **did not** want somebody to talk to her. Trust me on this. A club is one of the easiest places to meet a beautiful woman. Women in clubs are saying, "Here I am. What are you going to do?" Now women may say something like, "I'm not trying to meet anyone. I'm just here with my girlfriends." Yeah right. If someone they found appealing started talking to them, they would respond.

Parties, especially house parties, are good places to meet beautiful women. For one thing the atmosphere itself is more intimate. It is highly likely you and any of the beautiful women present know the party host or at least know one person in common. Before you have said one word you have a connection with a beautiful woman. Also, at a house party people are less pretentious, more likely to be friendly. When I attended a house party without a date, I always walked out with at least one phone number.

Parties in other locations should be looked at as a cross between a club and a house party. Whatever the case, gatherings such as these are easy places to meet beautiful women.

Work

Meeting beautiful women on the job is easy. Somebody usually introduces you. You might even share office space with her. Dating her is another thing though. Something to do with those silly sexual harassment laws. Seriously, since you have likely met the woman, this is the one place you can take your time to get to know her. She also gets a chance to know you better. The work environment is the one place where strict adherence to the rules is necessary. Slip up here can get you charged with sexual harassment. On the other hand you might have met your wife.

Before dating a woman on the job make sure

Rules For Meeting Beautiful Women

you are both clear as to what each of you want. Things can become problematic if you break off a relationship with someone in the office. The work environment is awkward and if she is vindictive she could charge you with harassment. The bottom line is when meeting and dating a beautiful woman on the job, be careful.

Organizations

Under organizations I would include churches, civic organizations, singles groups, etc. It's easy to meet beautiful women in different types of organizations. Keep in mind, however, with the exception of singles groups, women participating in different organizations are typically not looking for men, at least not within the organization. On the other hand as long as you follow the basic rules, you can easily get to know the women. Keep in mind the type of organization you are in. If it is a church, discussing going to a club probably won't help matters. In a political advocacy organization, it probably won't help if you don't have a sincere belief in the organization's position. The main thing to remember is when meeting women in organizations, follow the basic rules and adjust your approach in accordance with the goals of the organization.

Rom Wills

A Final Word on Men Approaching Women

Often a man will approach a woman on the street and start a conversation with her. During the conversation the woman will make it clear she has a man. Many men will respond, "What does that have to do with me?" **USE SOME COMMON SENSE!!!** If a woman tells you in the first five minutes of conversation she has a man she is basically saying she doesn't want you and she only spoke with you out of politeness. There are so many single women out there. Why do so many of y'all insist on trying to pick up a woman who **SAYS** she has a man? If a woman tells you she has a man wish her a nice day and move on. Let's for argument sake say she's interested in you anyway. Why would you want a woman ready to cheat on her man? **LEAVE THE ATTACHED WOMEN ALONE!!!** There are plenty of single women waiting for you. Stop playing games, learn to read the signals and go get these single women. Come correct or don't come at all.

Becoming Real

You now know the general traits which lead a woman to choose a particular man. The traits described are most common to the men in the select group. Men in the non-select group may have these traits as well though women may not think so. Women need to be stimulated on all levels. A woman has physical and material needs that must be satisfied. A woman's spiritual and emotional needs must be satisfied. Some men can satisfy a woman's physical needs while leaving her emotional needs unmet while other men can meet a woman's emotional needs. A man must meet both needs to fully satisfy a woman and keep her happy. Each category of man appeals to different needs in women. Mr. Goodbar and The Gamesman typically appeal to a woman's physical needs. The Masked Man and the Nice Guy appeal to a woman's emotional needs. The Real Man appeals to a woman's physical and emotional needs. Each group of men must take different measures to become more complete. The measures for each type are discussed below.

Nice Guys

There are two major problems with the Nice Guy. The most common is he either behaves like, or is perceived to be, a sucker. The Nice Guy is perceived as a man who does whatever a woman tells him to do. Here's an example: Fred is in love with Janice. He thinks she is the most beautiful woman in the world. They have been friends for a year. Fred drives her places, lends her money, shops with her, fixes things around her apartment, takes her out to expensive restaurants, and does anything Janice wants. Fred literally worships Janice. Janice on the other hand sees Fred as someone to spend some time with since the man she really wants, Todd, ignores her. Janice is not attracted to Fred in any shape or fashion despite knowing he is attracted to her. She considers Fred a pushover. Fred on the other hand is confused. He thought doing nice things for Janice would win her heart. He was taught to put a woman on a pedestal. Wrong.

The single biggest mistake a man can make with a woman is to put her on a pedestal. The same is true for a woman. She should never put a man on a pedestal. Women, no matter how nice and beautiful they may be, are still human. They make mistakes and most have done something questionable in their past. The first thing a Nice Guy has to realize is he must not put a woman's needs above his own. He must still treat a woman with respect, but it is not respect to be at her beck and call. The Nice Guy must demand respect for himself as well. Using the above example, Janice didn't respect Fred. If Janice respected Fred, she wouldn't let Fred do all those things for her knowing she didn't share his feelings.

Fred should have treated Janice as a friend once he realized she wasn't interested in him. Fred shouldn't have spent as much time trying to please her. If they talk, fine. If they hang out sometimes, fine. The key is not spending his time trying to please her.

I had a general rule of thumb when dealing with women in the past. If I wasn't getting what I wanted, I left the woman alone. This sounds harsh, women may call me a jerk, but you don't take from me and not give anything back. That doesn't work in my book. If you are supposed to be my friend and I'm not getting anything out of it, the friendship or whatever it was, is over. The Nice Guy must insist on getting what he is giving. He can't be a sucker.

The Nice Guy tries too hard to win over a woman who hasn't chosen him. Chris approached Joy and asked her out even though she didn't show any interest in him. After one date and a peck on the lips Chris thought he had met the woman of his dreams. He was ready to marry her despite not knowing anything about her. He didn't know whether she had a disease, anything about her goals in life, her spiritual beliefs, or whether she felt the same about him. He knew nothing. Over the next few weeks Chris did everything for Joy. He even respected that she didn't want to sleep with him before marriage. Chris did everything for her until he found out from someone he trusted that Joy was the biggest freak in town. She was using him for his money and found him repulsive. Chris was devastated. He had put her on a pedestal and gave to her without getting anything in return.

The second major problem with the Nice Guy is that he is generally not attractive to the women who meet him. He is typically not muscular and he dresses in a way which women don't consider sexy. Doris thought Tom was a nice man. She could talk to him about anything. She even thought he was somewhat handsome. Tom was even fairly confident and not a pushover. Despite his strong points Doris only saw Tom as a buddy. Why? Tom wore ill-fitting clothes and never exercised. He didn't do anything to make himself more appealing. Women have to enjoy looking at a man. He can have a great personality and still not get attention if he isn't physically appealing.

To become more ideal a Nice Guy must develop his confidence, aggressive nature, and his physical appearance. To develop his confidence the Nice Guy must first believe in himself. Every single man has something he is good at doing. For one man it may be writing. For another it may be cutting hair. The Nice Guy must find that talent and develop it. He must work to become good at that talent and then great. When someone feels like they are good at something they behave differently. They walk taller and they speak with authority on the area they are good at. They feel competent. The Nice Guy who develops his talents will feel confident because he knows he can do at least one thing well. This confidence will spread into other areas of his life because the principles used to develop skill in one area can be used in other areas as well. The Nice Guy then becomes confident in all areas of his life, including his relationships with women. The Nice Guy will no longer allow himself to be used by women or anybody else. He will become aggressive in life. He will no longer take bad treatment. He knows what he can do and knows what he won't stand for. He won't stand for shabby treatment on the job because he knows he can get another job. He won't allow a woman to take advantage of his kindness because he knows he can find a woman who will treat him the way he wants to be treated and give him the respect he deserves. When the Nice Guy becomes confident and aggressive, the same women who ignored him will start to want him.

Next the Nice Guy must work on his physical appearance. The Nice Guy must develop an exercise program and the discipline to stick to it. A big chest and smile takes a man a long way. The Nice Guy must dress to suit his physique. There are plenty of magazines a man can thumb through to get an idea about fashion. He can go to clubs and see what the players are wearing. The best thing, however, would be to ask women what they like. Women have always complimented me on the neckties I have worn. I pick out good neckties because I learned this talent from women. Women know what they like to see on a man. Don't be afraid to ask a woman in a clothing store how something looks on you.

The Gamesman

The Gamesman is the man who has suffered many rejections by women. Instead of getting his act together to become one of the select, the Gamesmen either avoids contact with women or plays games to get them. To become a Real Man the Gamesman must first stop playing games. It sounds simple but like most things it's not. Women have hurt the Gamesman. He knows as he really is the women will show little interest. So he pretends to be a part of the select. He has business cards printed. He spends all his money on one suit to go to clubs. He borrows his friend's car. He even pretends to own his friend's home. The Gamesman puts on a façade in his attempts to relate to women. Women usually see through the games. Yet women deal with Gamesmen because they are lonely or bored. Many women deal with the Gamesman because they are game players themselves. The Gamesman becomes trapped in a world where everything is illusion. The only way out of this world is to become a Real Man.

The Gamesman is creative. A man employs a lot of creativity to run game. The Gamesman uses his creativity to create situations where he looks attractive in a woman's eyes. There are a couple of steps a Gamesman can take to become a Real Man. The first thing a Gamesman must do is examine his own hostility towards women. Every man must do this because there is great power in having a positive attitude towards women. The Gamesman must look at all the times he was rejected by women and look at his own actions in causing the rejection. There was a lesson to be learned in each rejection. The Gamesman must go back and examine these rejections and determine what he should have learned. Alicia rejected Brian because of his looks, lack of ambition, and negative personality. Many women after Alicia rejected him for the same reason. Brian became hostile towards women as a result. He felt they were not accepting him. Brian made no attempts to change his personality. The proper course for Brian to take after Alicia rejected him would have been to examine the reasons why he was rejected. Brian would then work on the parts of his self that Alicia found unattractive. That way he would have been more attractive for the next woman.

The next major step for the Gamesman is to use the same energy that goes into running game and channel it into constructive activities. George is a former Gamesman who became a Real Man. George used to have phony business cards printed naming him as president of an import/export company. George constantly read information on the import/export business so he could seem like he knew what he was talking about. Women would give him play until they found out the truth. One day, as George was reading information about the import/export business, he realized it looked interesting so he decided to start a real business. In the process George became so focused on his business he stopped playing games and stayed away from women. After about a year the business took off. George went to a club to celebrate. He had no intention of passing out business cards.

He just wanted a drink and dinner to savor his success. To his surprise several women approached him, a few offered to buy drinks. All of a sudden he had charisma and instead of lying he could hand out his business cards with pride. His very aura had changed. He was no longer a Gamesman.

The Gamesman must let go of his hostility towards women and use his creativity to create something real.

The Masked Man

The Masked Man has developed the traits to become one of the select. He has the money, style, and appearance to attract beautiful women. He is on top of the world. After many relationships with beautiful women he has finally found the woman of his dreams. This woman falls in love with him and that's where the problems begin. Mark is a successful business executive with a Fortune 500 company. He has a big house, luxury car, and a six-figure salary. On top of this, he has great style and a slim muscular build. Michelle is a beautiful woman who modeled while in college and is now an attorney with a big firm. Michelle has the total package of beauty, brains, and being down to earth. Mark has hit the jackpot. He remembers the days when a woman like Michelle wouldn't even look at him. Mark used to be skinny and nerdy. He remembers when women used to play games with him. Mark remembers being stood up several times on dates. Despite his outward success Mark still carries those scars. Mark and Michelle get together and after a whirlwind romance get married. Michelle has always been open about her issues and has confronted them. In other words she doesn't wear a mask. Mark does wear a mask. Despite how much Mark loves Michelle even in marriage he wears his mask. Problems arise when the mask starts to crack. A small piece here and a small piece there. At one point, during a stressful moment, the mask comes off completely and Michelle doesn't recognize the man she married. Michelle sees Mark's true face and realizes she fell in love with an illusion. They divorce soon after.

Wearing a mask can get a man far in American society. He can hide his pain and his mask can project the confidence necessary to attract women and success. There is a price to pay for success in this manner. A Faustian bargain. A deal with the devil. The same mask that brings a man success will also prevent him from obtaining true happiness. We all want to be loved for who we really are and not the mask we wear in everyday society. The Masked Man wasn't loved for his real face thus the reason for the mask. When women fall in love with him they are falling in love with the mask. The Masked Man realizes if he wants to keep the woman he must also keep the mask on whenever he is with her. When he keeps the mask on like this for so long he loses sight of who he really is. The mask becomes such a part of him that even if he did remove the mask he finds that he has become the mask.

Although it may be painful, the Masked Man must keep the positive qualities of the mask but must gradually begin to take off the mask. Not an easy task. He may not attract as many women but he will attract his soulmate. A soulmate will never fall in love with your mask. The mask hides a man's spirit. To become a Real Man the Masked Man must have the courage to take off his mask.

Mr. Goodbar

Mr. Goodbar, Mr. Goodbar. Living every man's fantasy. His raw sex appeal and charm has the women swooning. Mr. Goodbar, the man who women step out on their husbands for. Mr. Goodbar, the man who doesn't spend money on dates. Mr. Goodbar, the man who should receive kickbacks from therapists because of all the hearts he's broken. Mr. Goodbar, the man who can get almost any woman but doesn't see the need because there are so many. Mr. Goodbar, the man who can't get the woman he really wants because she wants a Real Man and not a player. Sean has women serving at his beck and call. They give him money, buy him dinner, and do things with him they don't do with their boyfriends and husbands. Shelly, however, is different. Though she is attracted to Sean she has too much self-respect to be a part of his harem. She also believes she has better things to do than to try to change him. She wants a Real Man.

Ironically, it may seem easy for Mr. Goodbar to become the man that women want. He has many of the qualities anyway. All he has to do is pick one woman and settle down. That's the problem. Mr. Goodbar usually has women coming on to him blatantly. It's hard for any man to resist this type of temptation regardless of who he is. That's why there are so many stories of men from politicians to ministers getting caught with women other than their wives. The raw sexual power of women is hard to resist when fully aimed at a man. Mr. Goodbar is only human.

Despite the temptation there is a way for Mr. Goodbar to become a Real Man. Mr. Goodbar must practice sexual discipline. Mr. Goodbar must learn to say no. In many ways Mr. Goodbar is not in control of his life. He is bouncing around satisfying the sex drives of bored and frustrated women and his real needs might not even be met. Simon is a Mr. Goodbar who has been with more women than he can remember. Some of these women turned out to be dangerous. He has had his tires slashed, his home broken into, and even his mother has been harassed. He nearly lost a job because he rejected the advances of a female boss. Simon could have avoided this trouble if he had exercised good judgment with the women he chose to deal with.

A major problem with Mr. Goodbar and with the other categories of men is they don't realize the extent that the agenda of a relationship is set by women. Women choose the men and the men accept. Women are looking for certain things while men typically are looking for sex. Women always try to move their agenda along while men go along with this as long as the sex continues. This is especially a problem for Mr. Goodbar. He is thinking, "notch in the belt" while the woman is thinking he may be "Mr. Right." When women have this belief there is no telling what their reaction will be to rejection. Mr. Goodbar must always keep this in mind.

Instead of indulging a woman's fantasies Mr. Goodbar needs to exercise restraint. To do this he must develop discipline. The best way to develop this discipline is by engaging in projects that benefit him. He can work on a business or do community service. He can start reading conscious-raising books. These activities will redirect the sexual energy of Mr. Goodbar. Mr. Goodbar will find that once he starts exercising restraint in his sex life, other areas of his life become more productive. Most importantly he will become more attractive to the woman he really wants.

Sexual Chemistry

Now it's time to get down to the nitty-gritty. Let's talk about sexual issues. Sex is the one area that causes more trouble in a relationship than money or nosy girlfriends. Sex is really the major difference between a nice guy and a player. The most consistent statement by women about the nice guys is that they are not good in bed. If they were good in bed they wouldn't be nice guys. They would be called Mr. Right.

The nice guy has read through the previous chapters and learned some stuff and the player has read through thinking about what he could add. Both have taken the steps to improve themselves. So here you have a man who has worked out, bought some nice clothes, shined his shoes, and is more aggressive and confident. Women start to check him out. He manages to have sex with a woman. After they are through he is on top of the world because the woman was so fine. She would have had more fun watching paint dry. Despite the promise of a great night of passion she was left high and dry. Now what?

The sexual needs of many women are usually unmet **EVEN** when they are in steady relationships. Too many men only want to get theirs and may be fooled by women faking orgasms. The biggest single reason players get attention even when women know they are rotten is that the player is perceived to be better in bed than the nice guy. Now I can hear the nice guys now. "But I'm so romantic." "I make love in hotel rooms with rose petals and fine wine." "I take two hours in foreplay." Fellas, all of this is irrelevant if you don't turn on the woman to begin with.

One of the sad things about sexuality in American society is despite the fact that it's so much a part of our culture nobody really talks about what it really takes for satisfaction. It is especially sad that many relationships are destroyed because both men and women are not being satisfied. There are too many books out there about sexual satisfaction that to me are too clinical. Let me break it down for everybody. Sexual satisfaction by Rom.

There are two general rules that must be obeyed

by men to satisfy women at a minimum. First the woman must be **aroused** by the man and second, the woman must be **comfortable** with the man. Two simple concepts and yet if these simple concepts were understood relationships would be way more harmonious today. Let's look at each concept.

Arousal

The first factor necessary for a woman to be sexually satisfied is that she first must be aroused or, to put it simply, she must be turned on. A woman must be aroused before anything else can happen. When a woman is aroused her body goes through the changes necessary to prepare her body for sexual intercourse. Her breathing changes, her nipples become erect, her pulse quickens, and her vagina lubricates. Her body goes through chemical changes. The woman's body moves from an inactive state to an active state. Think of a clear, still pool of water. Now imagine that somebody has just dived in and caused some waves. That's what it's like for a woman to be aroused.

It is not easy for most men to arouse women. This is the nice guy's biggest problem. I have spoken with literally hundreds of women about why they are not attracted to nice guys. These women have had nice guys as friends who would do anything for them. It would seem logical for the women to date these men. The reasons women give for not dating these men always sound like this: "There was no chemistry." "He doesn't move me." "He's too nice." What women are really saying is the man is cool but they are not aroused enough to sleep with him. Even players won't get the ladies they can't arouse. A woman must be aroused before anything else can happen. There are two parts in the arousal process. First, the woman must find the man physically attractive. Second, the man must stimulate her mind. Most men usually emphasize one over the other. Few men are capable of doing both equally well. Some men do neither. Each part is explained below.

Physical Arousal

Sweet and simple, the man must be physically appealing to the woman. This doesn't mean the man has to look good to all women, just the one he wants. Every man is a Mr. Goodbar to somebody. To be physically appealing a man must work on his physique. A man's body doesn't have to be super muscular, just relatively fit. The man must wear clothing that fits well and compliments his body. The clothing should be kept up and clean. Clothing must be appropriate for the occasion. A man's face should always be well groomed. He should get regular haircuts and he should keep his facial hair neat and trim. If a man wears cologne it should be in an appropriate amount. Too little is a waste and too much is rather obnoxious. A man's voice must be pleasant and he must speak in an intelligent manner. He should practice his voice tones with a tape recorder. A man must walk in a confident manner. Overall, a man must have a strong physical presentation to arouse women.

A man must be healthy in order to maximize his potential to arouse women. Being healthy means both mind and body. The man must face and correct any emotional issues which may affect his ability to relate to women. Emotional issues affect how people look because these issues cause us to do destructive things to our bodies. We use drugs, abuse alcohol, and eat to excess. We don't keep our bodies clean inside and outside. This has a tremendous effect on the ability of a man to arouse a woman. A man with bad skin, crooked teeth, and dirty clothes won't get any quality women.

To arouse a woman, the man must appeal to all five of her senses. The man must look good to her. He must taste good to her when she kisses him. His voice must sound good to her ears. His skin must feel right to her. The man must smell good to her. The woman's senses must be aroused. The man who does this has his choice of women. The man who fails to do this will spend many nights alone.

Mental Arousal

A woman must be aroused mentally as well as physically. This is done through stimulating conversation, charm, and romance. Mental stimulation is intangible. A man can arouse a woman by being able to communicate an interesting subject to her. A man can arouse a woman by being able to make her laugh. Think about laughing for a second. What happens when people laugh? Their pulse races, their breathing changes. A woman who laughs moves from an inactive state to an active state. The same happens when a man surprises a woman with flowers or brings her a gift out of the blue. A woman is aroused when the man of her choice tells her she is beautiful in the morning despite her having on no make-up and bad breath. A woman is aroused when a man says things to make her feel good about herself.

A woman is also aroused by the actions of the men of her choosing. This means cooking dinner sometimes. This means washing the dishes. Taking care of her when she is sick. A man can arouse a woman by buying her groceries when she is broke. Fixing things around the woman's house can arouse her. A man can arouse a woman by simply keeping a promise. The man who treats his woman special always finds she is very appreciative when the time comes (smile).

Rom Wills

What Arousal Does for the Woman

A woman feels good when she is aroused. A man who can appeal to a woman's senses and mind will usually be chosen. An aroused woman is under a powerful influence. She is under romantic intoxication. Romance, when you break it down, is nothing more than a form of arousal. Those flowers, dinners, and getaways are designed to arouse women. Romance novels are popular for that reason. Romantic intoxication is worse than any other addiction. Women will change personalities while addicted to romance. They become more excited, their skin tingles, they get butterflies, and they begin to glow. Women have left their families, jobs, and friends to feed this addiction. A woman will sleep with her best friend's husband while romantically intoxicated. Players can keep a woman in a state of romantic intoxication. Nice guys fail to do this. A man skilled in the art of arousal, yes, it is an art, can manipulate a woman to the point where he can get anything he wants from her. Good, responsible men need to develop their arousal skills not only to keep their women happy but also to protect them from the more predatory players. The man who masters the art of arousing his woman need not fear competition.

Unfortunately, too many men don't feel it's their job to make women feel good. Too many men believe all they have to do is be responsible and stay out of trouble. They feel the woman is responsible for her own happiness. To some extent she is, but all women, regardless of how strong they think they are, need a man in their lives. And men need women. There are men out there who are confident, aggressive, and look good. They fail with women because they don't take any actions to make women feel good. Then they get mad at the women for not wanting them. Women want men who can make them feel good.

Women have dual sexual needs. Most women are only partially aroused because most men don't satisfy both physical and mental needs. This is why most women don't have orgasms on a regular basis. A woman must be fully aroused to reach orgasm. That's why many women have two men in their lives: The player to take care of their physical needs and the nice guy to take care of their mental needs. Arousal, however, is only the foundation for sexual satisfaction. The woman must also be comfortable during the sex act.

Sexual Comfort

A woman can be sufficiently aroused by a man and still not be satisfied with the sex act itself. Too often, a man may feel inadequate when the woman is not fully satisfied. He may feel his technique is sub par or he is lacking stamina. A cruel woman may make him feel like he is less than a man. There is something a man can do to satisfy the woman during sex that has nothing to do with techniques or even stamina. The man must be able to make the woman sexually comfortable.

To reach orgasm the woman must be able to "let go." Her inner feminine energy must be released. Women cannot release this energy when they are not comfortable. Many women have defense measures up to keep themselves from being hurt. They have a difficult time letting go. Women are at their most vulnerable when they release their inner feminine energy. The inner feminine energy is a receptive type of energy. It receives energy from the man. The sperm goes from the man into the woman. The release of the inner feminine energy triggers a woman's orgasm. Orgasm changes a woman's body so that it's possible to conceive a child. I have heard many women talk about how they knew the exact moment of their child's conception. They knew because of the nature of their orgasm. The inner feminine energy causes a woman to submit to the inner masculine energy of a man. A woman by being submissive in bed releases her true power. Most women don't have orgasms because they are reluctant to submit sexually to a man. Can we blame them?

Sexual Chemistry

It is a scary world out there for women sexually. When a man has sex he doesn't have any major concerns other than getting his. Many times a man may try to get away with having sex without protection. Women, on the other hand, have a lot to worry about. They have to worry about disease, pregnancy, an abortion if they get pregnant, and whether the man will be there if she keeps the baby. They have to worry about their reputations because "good girls don't do it." They worry if the man will stay around afterwards or try to dog them. This is happening during the sex act itself. There are even greater dangers for the woman.

Women have to be on guard against what I believe is their number one threat in sexual matters: sexual assault. This includes rape, fondling by strangers, and verbal abuse. An attractive woman walking down the street will have men staring at her, and, in too many cases, making suggestive comments. The men may high-five each other thinking they did something. The woman, though she may look cool, is probably scared to death. It is hard to find a woman who hasn't been the victim of some type of sexual assault. For one woman it may have been suggestive comments from a stranger. A stranger or even a friend may have fondled another woman. Another woman may have been a victim of incest. Sadly, many women have been raped not by strangers, but by men they know and trust. Some of the rapists are even their husbands and boyfriends. Forced sex is rape regardless of who the man is. When women have sex they want it with the man of their choosing and at the time of their choosing. Too many women are forced into sex, sometimes physically, sometimes through mental threats such as abandonment or withdrawal of support. Some male supervisors may use their position to get sexual favors from otherwise unwilling women. Hence the sexual harassment laws. Once a woman has been sexually assaulted the issues and trauma created will prevent a woman from willingly submitting sexually to a man no matter how handsome and loving he is.

A woman may also have trouble being comfortable enough to submit sexually to a man if she is uncomfortable with sharing her sexual past with him. If a man sleeps with 20 women he is considered "the man." He is a hero to the less fortunate men. If a woman sleeps with 20 men she is considered a slut. As a result of this double standard most women are not honest about their sexual history with the men they date. Too many men want a prim and proper woman who may have slept with a couple of men with whom she was involved in serious relationships. Men want to feel like they have the upper hand with their women. Many women, who probably forgot more about sex than some men know, have to act sexually innocent to

Sexual Chemistry

please the egos of their men. So women have to hold back. For instance, a woman already knows which position will satisfy her but she can't show the man because then he will know that she has more experience than she let on. Also this dynamic makes women ashamed of their sexual past if they slept with quite a few men. The woman will always be uncomfortable because she will worry about the man's reaction to her sexual experience.

Women will be uncomfortable with a man sexually if he is not handling his business. A woman is not going to be comfortable with a man sexually if the man is not doing his part to support the relationship. This is especially true when couples are living together. If the man isn't doing his part around the house or is not paying the bills on time, the woman is not going to be comfortable. If the man is unemployed and sitting around the house and his woman is doing everything from working to cooking to cleaning she is not going to be comfortable enough to have sex with him.

The man has to make the woman as comfortable as possible. The first thing he has to do is make sure they are in a comfortable environment when making love. This entails making sure the bills are paid if living together and that everything in the home is working correctly. The man has to make the woman feel like she is having sex on her own free will and not that she is forced to have sex because he spent $200 dollars on a date or that he will abuse her if she doesn't comply with his wishes. The man has to accept that she may have slept with several men in the past. Women have sex drives just like men. In fact, their sex drives may be stronger because their drives increase with age while men tend to lose their drives as they get older. A man has to communicate to a woman in words and actions that she can release her inner feminine energy with him. He has to be strong, responsible, and capable of fully arousing her. The woman must be comfortable sexually for her to be satisfied.

A woman must be aroused physically and mentally as a foundation for sexual satisfaction. She must be comfortable with the man to release her inner feminine energy. There is one final ingredient necessary to generate sexual chemistry with a woman. As the woman has to release her inner feminine energy the man must be able to release his inner masculine energy.

The Inner Masculine

Plenty of men are handsome, charming, and confident. These men get attention from the ladies because of these qualities. Despite these qualities, these men may still have trouble arousing woman. These qualities are important but more is needed. To generate sexual chemistry with a woman a man must be able to release his inner masculine. Men today are a mere shadow of what they could be. Many men are putting on a façade to get along in life. Many are wearing masks to conform to the social and political climate. This is especially the case when men deal with women. Men in the four categories behave this way. Mr. Goodbar plays to the sexual needs of women. The Masked Man hides his true face. The Nice Guy believes that women will come to him if he is nice enough. The Gamesman is busy playing games. All of these men are suppressing their inner masculine energy.

So what is the inner masculine energy? Let me break it down. Just as the inner feminine energy is receptive, the inner masculine energy is assertive. Sperm goes out from the man. The inner masculine is protective. It desires to protect those associated with it. The inner masculine is disciplined. The inner masculine is will power. The inner masculine faces its fears. Most men in American society suppress their inner masculine. As a result of political and social changes over the last few decades in American society, men are burying their true selves. Many men are not protecting their women and children. Many are abusing their families. Too many men are not assertive. They are passive in the face of everyday life. Many men are not disciplined. Many lack will power. A man in touch with his inner masculine will have a burning desire to control his own destiny. He will want to control his life. Which man in the four categories can truly say they control their life? Mr. Goodbar? His ego is in control. The Masked Man? He is afraid to show his true face. The Nice Guy? He is playing a game of make believe. He believes women should want him because he is so nice. The Gamesman? He is all about lies. The man who expresses his inner masculine is the Real Man. He is real because he expresses his true self.

Michael is a man who expresses his inner masculine. Michael left a well-paying job after being passed over for a promotion. Michael was also considered a troublemaker because he wasn't afraid to challenge bad decisions by the supervisors. Everybody thought Michael made a mistake but he couldn't stand working for another person. The corporate route was a means to an end. Michael's intention all along was to own a clothing store. He wanted to make his own rules and live according to his will. Through discipline and sheer willpower, Michael saved money and planned. Michael wanted to make a future for himself and his future wife and family. He knew that he couldn't do this if he was working for someone else and living according to their whims. The inner masculine causes a man to want to control his destiny.

All men should strive to express their inner masculine. There are several steps that must be taken.

Sexual Chemistry

The first thing a man must do is shed any facades he may be wearing. He must face the fears that cause him to wear the mask. A real man is a warrior. He has fears but he faces and conquers them. He must develop his will power. He must learn self-discipline. If he has any addictions he must gradually use his will power to cleanse himself. One man must quit smoking. Another man must stop abusing alcohol. Still another man must curb his sexual appetite. To express his inner masculine the man must learn to control himself. He must become his own master. When another man can control his destiny he is not his own master. When he abuses drugs or consumes beyond his means he is not in control. All men must strive to control their destiny.

I suggest all men develop their talents into a way to make money. This should be the case even if the man has a well-paying job. In the process of developing his talents into a moneymaking venture a man will discover that he is developing self-discipline and also creating something he can control. This small step can lead to something big where a man can truly control his destiny. Look at it another way. The man who has his own business and can control his destiny has plenty of women to choose from. These men typically arouse women, physically and mentally. Being in business for himself keeps the man in decent shape because he has to hustle. Any businessman has to be somewhat charming. To be successful, a businessman has to be responsible, which goes a long way towards making a woman comfortable.

A man in touch with his inner masculine will touch the inner feminine of the woman. Having the body, the charm, and a nice car is one thing, but if a man can stir a woman's inner feminine he has her hooked. Men, your work is cut out for you. If you want the woman then learn how to generate the heat.

Effect of Sexual Chemistry

Sexual chemistry literally changes a woman mentally and physically. The woman relaxes mentally and is generally in a more agreeable state. They walk and talk differently. They give out warm positive vibes. Arousal causes a change in a woman's hormones. These hormones change a woman's physical appearance. If she is slim she will begin to develop curves. Her breasts become fuller and her hips become rounder. If she is overweight she will lose weight and become shapelier. Women need sexual chemistry because of its positive nature. Is it any wonder why women go for the men who can arouse them?

Attitude Towards Women

An important ingredient in attracting women is having the right attitude towards them. In simple terms, a man must like women. A man must enjoy the company of women not only for sexual favors but also for their unique perspective. Unfortunately many men don't truly like women. These men have been hurt or emotionally abused by women and became bitter. These men only relate to women sexually if at all. These are the men who abuse women and talk poorly about them. Yet these men complain when the same women refuse to give them the time of day. No matter what a man says and does for a woman on the surface, his real attitude towards her reflects in how he looks at her, his body language, and in the vibes he gives off.

We have all been hurt in life. Nothing is wrong with being hurt. Nothing is wrong with being knocked down. There is something wrong in staying down. Every knockdown is a learning experience. Too often we fail to learn the lesson. The women he tried to meet constantly rejected James. They would talk to him for a few minutes and then walk away. James became bitter towards women and began to think they were stupid and no good. James' problem was that he would come on too strong. He would stand too close to women. He didn't make them feel comfortable. If he thought about his actions he might have realized his mistakes. Instead of doing this, he blamed the women. He didn't see any flaws in himself. The first time he was rejected he should have thought about the incident and not have made the same mistake again.

Women have rejected every man, including Mr. Goodbar. There are always two directions a man can take. He can become bitter and develop animosity towards women or he can learn from each rejection. Every time he was rejected Julien would go over in his mind everything about the incident. Each time he would correct the problem. Julien got to the point where women couldn't easily reject him. The most important thing Julien did was he always kept a positive attitude towards women. He realized that the rejections were God's way of making him into a better person. Every rejection must be seen as a shaping force that will prepare the man for his soulmate.

Women as Sex Objects

A man must learn to see women in a different light. Many men do not want a real woman. They want an object who's pretty with a slamming body. Men want the image of a perfect woman. There is nothing wrong with wanting a beautiful woman. The Creator made us that way. A man must, however, remember beautiful women are real people with real feelings. When most men see a beautiful woman they see a conquest, an object to be acquired. The man, in his quest, is not thinking about the woman's emotional well-being. She is seen as a possession to be discarded once he is tired of her. Mr. Goodbar does this all the time. The Masked Man learns to do this. The Nice Guy and Gamesman wish they could do this. The problem with this is while men are looking for the perfect woman, they are passing up the real women who are right in front of them. Ironically, Nice Guys are especially guilty of passing up decent women in their search for a perfect woman. I have met many Nice Guys who have wondered why beautiful women reject them. These same men will ignore women right in front of them who may be overweight or too slim, or unattractive on the surface. The Nice Guys will ignore their female equivalent in their pursuit of the perfect woman.

Men have to take a look at their attitude about women. Women are not mere objects. They are real people with the same imperfections as men. This may seem obvious but it is not. It is rare that men reject women on character issues. Physical attractiveness is important, but unless you are drop-dead fine and she is just too ugly to bear, don't look for perfection. Don't put women on the pedestal of perfection. Don't look at her as an object to be possessed. She is a real person. She has things she worries about. Asking women to live up to a perfect image is too much for many women to handle. That's why many of them are on these crazy diets, have breast implants, fake hair, and fake eye colors. Men have to learn to accept women as they are, within reason. Never accept bad behavior from a woman. Look for women with good character. She may be overweight or not as sexy but with the right type of love she can transform into a traffic stopper.

Mental and Spiritual Development

Quinton is confident and aggressive. He has a buffed body, dresses well, and has a well-paying job. This man attracts many women to him and he is able to wine and dine them and is great in bed. Quinton is a Mr. Goodbar. Despite everything Quinton has going for him, he can't keep a woman for the long term. Quinton is able to satisfy a woman's physical and material needs. When it comes to deeper philosophical and spiritual issues, Quinton is lacking. Quinton can't discuss issues deeper than his job, sports, and the hottest music and TV shows. Women find relationships with Quinton to be shallow. Despite Quinton's sex appeal, women begin to look for men who can satisfy their mental needs in addition to their physical needs. Many women keep Quinton as a sex object and nothing else. Quinton, despite the attention he gets, is tired of this situation. He wants a full relationship with a special woman. There are steps he can take to secure this type of relationship.

Just as a man must develop himself physically, he must also develop himself mentally. Too many men don't read anything other than the sports section and fashion magazines. Too many men are limited on the opinions they can offer intelligently in a conversation. Women are drawn by a man's physical appearance. They are, however, turned off immediately if the man opens his mouth and sounds stupid. Only women who are interested in sex want an inarticulate, stupid man. Women want good conversation from men. I have heard many women complain about meeting attractive men who were stupid. They'll say, "He was cute and all, until he opened his mouth." Unless you are a male stripper and she's horny, a man has to be articulate and knowledgeable. A man should take the following steps.

A man should go to a bookstore and head right to the non-fiction sections. Pick up books on philosophy, psychology, politics, history, or anything non-fiction. I highly recommend books that contain ideas that go against your belief systems. This causes you to actually have to think about something. Once a

Mental and Spiritual Development

man begins to think his consciousness grows and demands new ideas to feed this consciousness. These new ideas will lead to the man formulating his own ideas. These ideas want an outlet. The man will automatically develop ways to effectively communicate his ideas. He will even begin to look different as he becomes more confident in expressing himself. Women will respond to this. A man can be drop-dead fine and get plenty of attention from women and still lose out in the long term if he isn't able to truly think and express himself.

Spiritual development

Every man must acknowledge the presence of a higher power. Whether you want to refer to this higher power as God, Allah, Jehovah, Buddha, or the Creator, we have to realize there is something out there greater than we are. I'm not going to suggest which spiritual path to follow. Each man has to find his own way. For some that may be in a church while for others it may be solo study. He must realize that his actions must be in accord with the higher power. A man must realize by intentionally causing pain or engaging in unethical conduct he is going against God. Men who lie to women or play games are engaging in unethical conduct. They are getting sex by deception. This deception causes pain to the woman and ultimately her soul. This type of transgression will cause a man to lose out on many blessings. A man must be righteous! Let's use sex as an example. A man can still pursue sex, but he has to be honest with himself and the woman. If he knows he only wants sex from a woman he needs to make this clear to her. He shouldn't pretend he loves her if he doesn't. If the woman doesn't like this arrangement the man needs to respect her decision. The man must always be correct in his dealings with women.

A man must develop all aspects of himself. He can't just develop his body and his financial and material package. He must develop his mind and he must establish a connection to the Creator.

The Real Man

Now it's time for the man reading this book to put everything together. He knows that women choose the men. He is now aware of the signs the women generally show when they have chosen a man. The man is aware of the physical and mental traits that attract women. He now knows the basis of true sexual satisfaction. Each category of man has a portion of the traits necessary to attract women. Mr. Goodbar has the sex appeal and the charm. The Masked Man has the financial ability and the status. The Nice Guy has the virtues. Even the Gamesman has some creativity. The Real Man has the traits of all of these groups, which he uses to positively enhance his life, his woman's and his community.

Rom Wills

One thing that must be understood is that women go for the man who has the best package. Craig is good-looking but not movie star fine. When he is in a room full of women he will draw more attention than all the pretty boys put together. Why? Craig has the total package. He is good-looking with a good build. His clothes compliment his body. His head is held high and he exudes a powerful confidence. His gaze is steady and his voice, though soft-spoken, commands attention. The man looks like he can handle any situation. He has a magnetic presence that draws all eyes to him. He is a Real Man down to the core of his being.

People may think this man is a fantasy figure. I disagree. These men are all over the place in American society. In the African-American community in particular there is one group of men that has an overrepresentation of Real Men. These men are commonly referred to as "conscious brothers." The conscious brother is the man who may be selling books on a street stand. The conscious brother is the man wearing dreadlocks proudly in a corporate environment. He is the man who once sold drugs for profit who now writes poetry and dispenses knowledge of self for free. The truly conscious brothers are Real Men because they are true to themselves. They are not Uncle Toms or gangsters. They are not undercover gigolos or males not man enough to make commitments. They are not perfect but they realize this and strive to shake off the chains of mental slavery. They are not studs going from woman to woman for gratification. They are not men pretending to be nice and polite because society told them this will get the women. The conscious brother is real.

The typical conscious brother is balanced. They are usually physically appealing and by being conscious they have also developed or are in the process of developing their minds. They realize that there must be a balance in life and that a Real Man does not suppress who he is to conform to others. The conscious brother realizes he must be self-disciplined because that is what it means to be a man.

There are other examples of Real Men in other communities, races, and economic classes in America. Unfortunately there are not enough. In American society we have too many pretenders. We have men who make enormous salaries and yet act like little boys. We have men whose sole purpose is to keep women sexually satisfied. I have seen so-called men who have played malicious games on women and then cry like little boys when they got played. I have also seen the Real Men in American society. These men will take their time and energy to make a difference in the lives of the women and children around them. Some of these men are recognized, many are unsung heroes. We need more of these men in society.

The Real Man has developed his body and his mind. He uses his talents to provide a living for himself and he is an asset to the larger community. The Real Man also realizes that all gifts flow from a higher power. The Real Man is mindful of his blessings and the responsibility that comes with those blessings.

The Real Man knows he must have a Real Woman. There are plenty of women game players out there. Many women are scandalous. The Real Man does not indulge the games and fantasies of these women. The aura and power of a Real Man repels these women. The Real Man looks for the woman who is real herself and ready for bonding on physical and spiritual levels. The Real Man and Real Woman can then grow together until it is time for their souls to reunite with the Creator.

Becoming a Real Man is what every man should strive for. The journey may be short for some and long for others but it is a journey that must be taken.

To the men reading my words I issue a challenge. Strive to become real. Throw off the masks you have worn to survive in this society. Return to your true self. You were not born to be a sex toy. You were not born to be a money machine. You were not born to be a doormat. You were not born to be a trickster. You were born to make a difference. You were born to protect women, not compete with them or abuse them. You were born to raise children and not ignore them, leaving them to fend for themselves. You were not born to hang out at a liquor store or beg someone else to take care of you. You were not born to be defined by others. You were born to control your destiny. You were born to be aggressive and disciplined. You were born to be a warrior. You were born to be a man. Women have been patient with you. It is now time to live up to your destiny.

Peace.

About the Author

Rom Wills is a 1987 graduate of St. Joseph's University in Philadelphia, Pennsylvania and a 1990 graduate of the Washington College of Law, The American University in Washington, D.C. He has written articles about politics and relationships for several Internet sites and print media.

Rom is the founder of E.R.L. Publishing.

For comments write Rom at:
E.R.L. Publishing
P.O. Box 4071
Arlington, VA 22204

or

erlpublishing@aol.com

Visit E.R.L. Publishing at:
Http://hometown.aol.com/romwills/erlpublishing.html